T0145297

MY FOOTBALL STORY

Written and Illustrated by: D. Collins

© 2020 D. Collins. All rights reserved.

No part of this book may be reproduced, stored in a retrieval system, or transmitted by any means without the written permission of the author.

AuthorHouse™ UK
1663 Liberty Drive
Bloomington, IN 47403 USA
www.authorhouse.co.uk
UK TFN: 0800 0148641 (Toll Free inside the UK)
UK Local: 02036 956322 (+44 20 3695 6322 from outside the UK)

Because of the dynamic nature of the Internet, any web addresses or links contained in this book may have changed since publication and may no longer be valid. The views expressed in this work are solely those of the author and do not necessarily reflect the views of the publisher, and the publisher hereby disclaims any responsibility for them.

Any people depicted in stock imagery provided by Getty Images are models, and such images are being used for illustrative purposes only.
Certain stock imagery © Getty Images.

This book is printed on acid-free paper.

ISBN: 978-1-7283-7900-5 (sc)
ISBN: 978-1-7283-5684-6 (e)

Print information available on the last page.

Published by AuthorHouse 09/08/2020

authorHOUSE®

To all my readers,

I hope my story inspires you to continue doing what you enjoy. I believe sport, especially football, is good for all boys and girls. There is so much support and resources out there to help all kids enjoy all sports, so don't give up on your dream. I hope one day I can tell you the rest of my story. This is a true story about my football in the early days of my life.

I would like to thank Ray, the football scout, for believing in me. I hope one day I see him again to say thank you. It was a shame I was not open about my anxieties.

A huge thank you to Lisa for your love and support.

From the age of four, I loved playing football. I would kick the ball up the wall because it always came back to me how I wanted it to. So the wall became my best friend when my brother or no other kids were around to play with me.

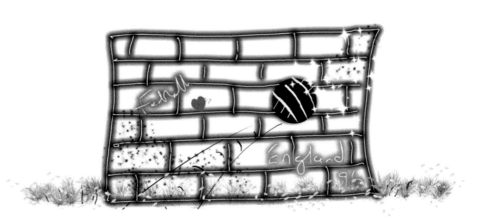

Every day I thought about football.

Football was really in my heart. I even dreamed about football and becoming a real footballer.

When I played matches, I scored lots of goals. Everybody would cheer, and that made me feel happy.

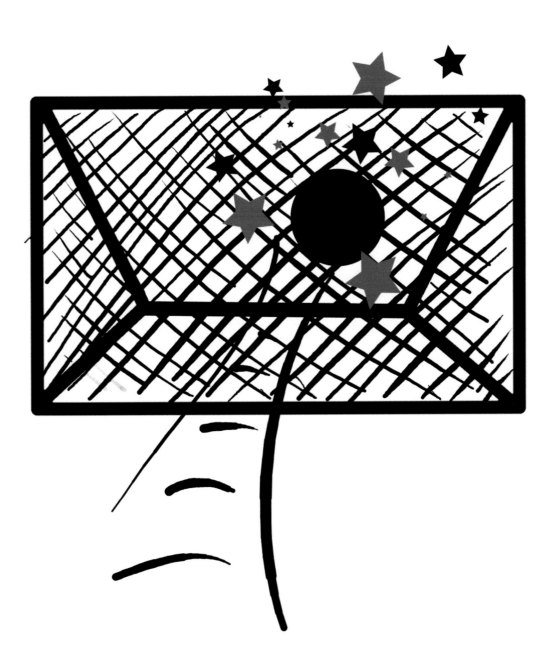

In school I played for two football teams. I felt very lucky.

On some match days, all the team would go into the changing room and get ready for the match. I felt very excited about the matches. But I was never able to get dressed with the rest of my team, and this made me feel sad. I always arrived for matches already dressed in my kit.

My team friends were always kind to me; even my brother was on the team. But I could not even be with him to get ready for the matches. I liked being with my brother.

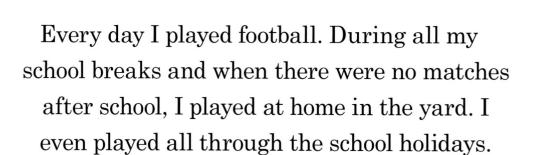

Every day I played football. During all my
school breaks and when there were no matches
after school, I played at home in the yard. I
even played all through the school holidays.

Sometimes when I didn't have a football because
I had lost it or it had deflated, my brother and
I would pretend we were in the Olympics.

We did lots of sports. When I was around 10 years old, I was on the cricket team, the chess team, and two school football teams. I won top sports all-rounder of the whole school. I felt very proud to win that trophy. But football was what made me the happiest. It was what I loved and was the sport that was in my heart.

When I was ten years old, my brother, some teammates from school, and I all went to sign up for a new club called the Panthers. Everyone was so excited. But this day turned out to be a really sad one for me as I was unable to sign up for the club. All the team was disappointed. And I was very upset.

My brother was so proud of me and started speaking to the man there about me. He put his arm around me and said to the man, "She's my brother."

The man looked so shocked and said I could not sign up because I was a girl.

I cried for many days because of this.

On match days with the boys, they would call me Dennis. And when I played with the girls, they called me by my real name, Denise.

All the school's boys' teams knew I was a girl, but all the teams we played against did not know. This was the only way that I could play more football and the only way I could play on the boys' team.

I was a super footballer! Why did it matter that I was a girl?

I then started to get upset about going to the big school because it was a girls' school. I thought my chances to play football would be less.

My mum then telephoned the local newspaper which printed a story about me and a picture of me. It led to someone writing to me from Millwall football team, asking me to come down. I never replied. I let my travel sickness and my anxieties get the best of me. I should have asked for help with these feelings and thoughts because that would have helped me overcome my worries. So please, if you worry about anything, talk to your teacher, brother, sister, father, mother, or another trusted adult.

I continued playing in the school teams until I went to my secondary school, where my football continued.

I hope one day I can share the rest of my story with you.

ABOUT THE AUTHOR

I grew up playing football in poverty-stricken East London, where the yard was my football pitch.

I started playing football once I left nursery. Football was all I cared about right up to my teenage years. This is a true short story about the beginning of my football journey.

TEAM PHOTO